A

Secret

Lie

How the

World "Really" Is!

by:

Jason Judkins

About The Author

Follow Me On:

Facebook:

http://www.facebook.com/ASecretLie

On Twitter:

http://www.twitter.com/ASecretLie

Email: asecretlie@gmail.com

www.asecretlie.com

This book is dedicated to fighting corruption and inequality in all forms at all levels, and also to challenge conventional thinking.

Contents

CONTENTS (CONTINUED)

Advisory

The author of this book, Jason Judkins, is not a licensed professional in the subject matter covered. The contents are opinion and based on the author's life experience. The author assumes no liability or responsibility from the consequences of reading this book! Read at your own risk!

Preface

People you know in your life die all the time, at any age. So I thought, what if I died suddenly? How would my kids know what I want them to know to be successful in life? Of course they have their mother and other family to help them grow up. But they might not know what I know, agree, remember, or be able to articulate it.

Then I thought, there's probably somebody in this situation now! Some kids don't have parents, only have one parent, or have both parents but aren't told everything THEY need to know.

This book talks about "real world" life! The things that everybody thinks but would never talk about. Because if people really said what they thought, it could hurt their status at work, in family, and in the community. Life is a game and you better know the rules to succeed! This book is the truth, as I know it.

Chapter 1:
The World We Live In

The world we live in is full of CRAP! Full of it! Nobody wants to do what I would call physically hard, low pay, no benefit, crappy work, but wants to tell everybody else it's good for them. Everybody wants the easy, high paying, highly respected job. Now there are exceptions to every rule. So people are always trying to pass down work from the top to the bottom. Until you have the person who will do it. Everybody says they love to work, Wrong! Only if it's the work they want to do, or if they absolutely have to work. I would love to see the person who says they love to work dig ditches for a living on minimum wage and still say they love it.

You can take most of life mantras and flip them around. Like, "Beauty is only skin deep" or "Beauty is in the eye of the beholder." Basically trying to be nice to ugly people in telling you looks don't matter. I hate to tell you but looks do matter!! That's why sex sells in advertising. So, look as best as you can! It might determine if you get a certain job, spouse, or something as simple as getting a favor somewhere. Now don't do anything harmful to your health to look good! Like making yourself throw up. Your health is way more important than your looks but again, looks do matter! For example, I've seen one-person walk in, ask for a job, and the employer said they're not hiring. Later that day a hot chic walks in the door and all of a sudden they're hiring. All of a sudden the employer had a change of mind of needing to hire more employment?

This is just one of many examples of how this world is run by people, not absolute laws, magical outside forces, or anything else. I know this sounds like common sense. But people always say, "That boss, judge, employer, policeman, politician, pastor, boyfriend, girlfriend, etc, can't do that. Well they can and do. The faster you learn that, the better off you'll be! Then people say,

"What goes around, comes around," like a hidden force is at work. That is simply not true and it evidently hasn't stop people from mistreating each other. Except breaking the law, which does bend for some people. You have no rights. You're allowed whatever rights the government allows you to have, and they can be taken away at any time. True rights cannot be taken away. Of course government has its limits too. You also have to remember when reading this book that one person's perception of reality is different from another persons. Some people can read this book and think that just because they have things good, life is good for everybody. You can have one person who is the star athlete and everybody wants to do for this person. While at the same time you have some poor loser who nobody wants to do anything for. Even though these two people live on the same planet, they're going to perceive the world two different ways. I guess that's why people say to walk in someone's shoes before you judge them.

I'm sure you've heard, "We Are All Created

Equal," Wrong! Some people are born stronger, more beautiful, wealthier, healthier, etc.. You get my point! And you're darn sure put on a vertical scale the second you go to work! We're all created equal until we go to work! People also have one set of rules for their kids, and another for everybody else. Everybody has a pretty clear-cut view of what's right and what's wrong, but that view tends to change when it's dealing with their own kid. You always hear how somebody thinks this person did wrong or that person should go to jail, but that changes when it's your own child. It's just human nature. But that shows you how much of an advantage or disadvantage somebody has just based on who their parents are!

I think I've always pretty much have viewed myself no better or no less than anybody else. There are the social classes out there, rich, middle, and poor. Everybody pretty much sticks to his or her social class. I never really understood that until I got older. Jesus said the messenger is no less than the person sending the message. Meaning we're all equal and should treat each other in such a manner. But it just doesn't exist for the most part.

Everybody wants to be part of a group and have friends. 90% of these people will push aside their core values to not ruin their group status, very sad!! It's basically peer pressure. What we're taught to avoid in younger years, but people buckle to peer pressure their whole lives. I've always viewed myself more as a leader than a follower. You're taught though life to "be yourself" and "people should accept you the way you are." This simply is not true either. In real life you're taught to fit a certain mold and if you break away from that, you're a weirdo.

There is a guy who wrote a poem about "wearing mask," and how his whole life was a front. He felt like he had to be a different person and change who he is, depending what environment he was in at the time. And he's looking for the one person who will accept him for who he really is. I couldn't relate to this poem when I got it as a teenager. But as I got older, I felt like I had to put on a mask going into different situations. That my whole life was going from one mask to another. It's hard not to be yourself! It actually takes work. I can't stand to talk to fake people! So you do have to wear mask in life. It's better to just go ahead and con the person as they're coning you, talking in a work sense. You should always be open and honest with you family.

This second point is just as equally as important as the first! First being the whole world is Crap! Most everything in life is determine by the natural laws of "Supply and Demand." It's a force of nature. It cannot be stop, it just happens. It determines how much an apple cost, how much you'll be paid at a job, to what spouse you have, generally speaking. I got trapped in thinking when I was younger, that there was some type of magic that would set my life in motion. As far as a job, spouse, etc.. That opportunity would just find me. As I've gotten older I've found everything takes work, everything! Unless you win the lottery. If you want a job, YOU have to make it happen. If you want a spouse, YOU have to make it work. If you want a hot body, etc.. So opportunity doesn't come out of chance, it comes from some previous work YOU did. Nobody will really do anything for you in life, other than maybe your parents. So who you're born to has a lot to do with how hard you'll have to work to get to a destination.

Another one is, "Honesty is the best policy." I do believe you should always be honest with your family, but not when it comes to work and everyday situations. A guy I used to work with was smoking on his job when he wasn't suppose to. He came off his forklift and the manager asked him if he had just been smoking. The employee said yes. He was fired and immediately walked off his job. That day I thought, so much for telling the truth! It just got that guy fired. Your employer can't prove probably half of what gets you in trouble. A lot of what gets you in trouble is by your own admittance. You have to be careful what you say to your employer. Employers lie to their employees all the time, its just life. One thing about life is that you have to learn how to read people. Not what they're saying but what they're thinking, kinda like a poker game. You have to be able to read between the lines when people are talking to you. You should always be honest when under oath, that can get you in a lot of trouble!

"Actions speak louder than words." People are supposed to judge you based on your actions, not your words. But in reality, it's just the opposite. People are so easily bullshitted! People get lied to over and over again by the same person, and yet the person always believes him/her. Like something has changed. This just shows you how stupid and gullible people really are. People always want to believe the best in people and that they're not lying to them, when this just isn't reality.

Another one is people tell you to be yourself. But people are always trying to act like somebody else. Or trying to look like somebody else. Most people really don't like people for who they really are, they like people for what they can do for them. Our society really doesn't respect or honor a person's individuality. We want everybody to fit this mold of getting married, working 8-5, having kids, going to church, looking a certain way, etc.. But if you want everybody to do the same thing, how is that not socialistic? I think individuality goes hand-to-hand with freedom.

I think one reason the world is full of crap is because; the people at the top, who influence others, know how things really are. But try to project a good image so others will follow it and make life better for everybody. I think this is good for kids but at some point you have to grow up. This is one difference of the 1950's and now. In the 1950's people had all of the same problems as today but didn't talk about them. They just put on a happy face and acted like everything was perfect. When somebody asked if something was wrong, they would just lie and say everything was fine. Contrast that with today of how things are more open. Which way is better? Probably neither. Almost like if man continues on its current path, we'll end back like Sodom and Gomorrah. It's probably why things go in cycles.

Preachers are always talking about GOD giving us dominion over the earth. That you must plant your seed, let it harvest, and grow. Takes me back to having to grow up. GOD gave YOU dominion. Nothing is given to you here. You have to go and take it from somebody else. I'm not talking about stealing. I'm saying you have to stand up and get things yourself. Saying if you don't take opportunity, somebody else will! And if people don't give you your dominion, don't respect you, and don't respect your decisions. Forget about them, even close people too. Cause it's your life and they should respect that. But be careful of the decisions you make. You don't want to make a mistake that causes you to run back to the same people. If that happens, these people have every right in telling you how to live.

People will say this person or that person is selfish. Well most people are selfish. Cause it's their own life and they're going to do what they want to do. It makes sense really but some people can't comprehend that people are just involved in things for their own self-interest.

People always want to change somebody else, their family, friends, etc.. You can't change hardly anybody! You can only educate people but they have to make up their own mind. Accept that and move on. You go on and live YOUR life. You can only change what's in your control, not others.

You hear people talk about how somebody is rich and that they give money but that they could give more. The person replies that you have to have things like a house, car, etc. What am I supposed to do, sleep on the ground? Well Jesus did. Jesus didn't own a house or a car. Jesus is the one who gave it all. I not trying to discourage people from giving, I'm just making a point.

Chapter 2:
Religion

This is my least favorite chapter to write!
Cause I do view Religion as a positive force in
the world. But like everything else, there are
pitfalls to watch out for. I don't know if
religion is 100% real or not? Nobody does. I
have never met God or Satan. I have never
been to Heaven or Hell, unless it was in
another life. The missing parts are where
your personal faith and views come in the
equation. What I do know is that Christianity,
for the most part, is preached and not
followed.

My views on Christianity are; If Jesus is the
example to live by, then his word is the most
important part of the Bible. I say that cause
people always want to point to other parts of
the Bible, outside the Gospels; to parts that
justify what that person is doing or not doing.
And if Jesus is the example to live by; he slept

on the dirty ground and didn't have a car. I don't see too many people doing this. Jesus repeatedly talked negatively about rich people and repeatedly championed the poor. So how can a rich person be a Christian? Because they tithe their 10% and get to keep the other 90%? That is Old Testament law. If a woman was rapped, she has to marry the guy who rapped her. That is also Old Testament law but we didn't keep that one. I've also heard it's ok to be rich and a Christian, as long as you're a good steward of your money. Well, of course who determines that? It would seem to me that the goal of a Christian would to be poor. Since the love of money is evil. I don't have anything against rich people if they earned their money fairly and if the next person can earn it just as fairly. I do have a problem with rich people who tell everybody else what he or she should do, or believe, while they do what they want. I also have a problem with rich people who become rich and then do things to keep other people from becoming rich like them. It's my personal opinion that the four gospels are about all you need! I don't think Jesus left anything out of how we should live our life in the Gospels. It's the other books of the Bible that give people justification for how THEY want to live. If Jesus is the example, do you think Jesus would ever buy a Mercedes? I don't, cause Jesus never really owned anything. The Bible also talks negatively about debt. But the majority of people run out and get into as much debt as they can.

You always hear how America is a "Christian Nation." This, for the most part, is not true either. Christian principles are found in the basis for a lot of our laws. A lot of our founding fathers were Christian. Ben Franklin, Thomas Jefferson, and Thomas Paine are the more prominent Agnostics. Thomas Jefferson wrote his own Bible, taking out all of Jesus' miracles. We are told we have a "Separation of Church and State." What we really have is a "Separation of Church and Work." I have had many jobs! I have never felt like I have worked for a real Christian. I've worked along side a few Christians but never felt like I had one for a boss. I've never had a boss get out his/her Bible to see what he/she should do in a work situation. I almost think you can't be in management and be Christian. You have to lie too much! You have to do what the person paying you wants you to do. That's when the Bible gets tossed and the person will just ask for forgiveness the next day.

When I was younger, I thought being a Christian Nation; business would promote good Christian people over drug users, liars, adultery's, drunks, gays, etc.. That simply is not true! All employers care about is who does the best job and who will do whatever they're told to do. They could care less if you are a sinner but we're a "Christian Nation!" Shows who business really promotes!

The one thing you CANNOT be in life is lazy! You can steal, cheat, drink, do drugs, etc.. All of these things can be looked passed as long as you work and say you're sorry. But if you don't work and do these things like everybody else; you might as well go live in a hole! That is the ultimate sin! Well it's ok to be lazy if you're rich, but you can't be lazy if you're poor. Actually, it's ok to be any of the above sinners if you're rich! But if you're one of the above and poor, then you're a piece of shit!

Religion is a front for a lot of people. It's a "go with the crowd" type thing. I'd say 80%-90% of the people in the world are go with the crowd. If rich people really believe in Christianity, they would socialize with people outside their social class, creed, etc.. Some do but a lot don't.

There are stories of people who have had near death experiences and have gone to the afterlife and back. They name objects and recall conversations in operating rooms that they would have no way of knowing. I do want to believe these people. It's probably the only "real" evidence I have for Religion, Christianity, or an afterlife.

I know that nobody's perfect and we all sin. We're not suppose to judge others, and that this whole book is a judgment. I write this chapter cause I got caught up in the Christian message in my younger years. I thought if I was a Christian, and was doing the "right" thing. It would get me ahead in life. I found the people who claim to care, most of the time really don't. What a let down that was! You can tell what a person really thinks by how they treat their money!

In listening to these people, I probably missed out on some fun times I'll never get back. I final realized these people were telling me not to do something, while they turn right around and do it themselves. I was also too scared to do stuff in fear of going to Hell. I feel sorry for kids these days being told about Hell. That's a lot for a little kid to take in! I think it's done so kids won't do drugs, drink, and other sins. Which is a good thing but has other consequences too. If there were no Hell, nobody would go to church.

I know people from my past that started going to church. I thought, let me see if this person has changed. Most of the time it's the same person that hasn't changed. If you go to church and you think you're better than everybody else cause you're rich, even with others in your own church, well then you're not really a Christian to me. I really think that rich Christians think that God approves of whatever they do cause they have money. I think they think it's ok to tell other people what they're doing is wrong even if they do it themselves. Cause I think they think since God gave them lots of money it's ok for them to drink, smoke, lie, etc.. Cause if God disapproved of them doing it, then they wouldn't be rich. So this makes rich people better than everybody else. Basically if a rich Christian gets drunk, it's ok cause God made them rich and will forgive them. But if you're poor and do this, then you'll go to Hell.

You ever notice when arguing with people, they'll never admit you're right or that they were wrong? No matter how many facts are against them? Kinda goes with how most people can't say they're sorry about something. That makes me think, what's the point in arguing? Most people won't change what they think, some do slowly. For people to really listen to your views, you have to be a very accomplished person. But I find most of what these elite tell you is not all truth. They keep what they really think to themselves, a lot of the point of writing this book. What other people have, their money, knowledge, power, etc, is not for you or your kids. It's for them and their kids.

Its amazing how mass amounts of people can be so easily brainwashed. I guess because we all come into the world with nothing. We have to be taught what we know from somebody. Everybody has to get their news from somewhere. And no matter where you get it from, it will have a slant to it. I gotta tell ya; the right-wing media brainwashes you just like the left-wing media does. I hate to say that you probably get more truth from comedians and rappers than you do from school, politicians, clergymen, news, etc..

One problem with belief I have is that people think they have some supernatural being watching over them. I do believe in miracles but how could a true, just, equal, and all knowing God show favor to me when people are starving to death in the world? So this makes me think God has very little involvement in our daily lives. Which goes back to the point of everything being up to

YOU to do!

You hear a lot of how God blessed America. I would agree with that when you look at all the natural resources America has. We have, I believe, just about every resource available. Most countries have to import many of their resources, which makes them dependent on someone else. And when you depend on somebody else, you're not truly free. As far as everything else America has cause God blessed us? I'd equally argue that we are at where we are because people stood up to oppression and won. And the minute we stop standing up to oppression, oppression will return. It's just natural though history that one group of people oppress another. I just don't want us to fall in a trap that since God blessed us, we don't have to worry or really do anything cause God will take care of us. You're always one generation away from losing your freedoms. It's always something that will have to be fought for.

Another one people say is that, "God will never give you more than you can handle." This in itself sounds stupid and oxymoronic.

First, there's no way to prove or disprove it. Next, evidently anything that happens to you, you can handle it. So if you get in a car wreck, God decided you could handle that. So he gave you one? Just another saying people use to brainwash you with. Just like how everything happens for a reason. Somebody gets in a car wreck and dies, what's the reason behind that? I guess others can learn from that? Doesn't do anything for the person who died. I think just sometimes things happen, that's it. People say you shouldn't live in the past but everything happens for a reason. So which one is it? If you're thinking of why something happened the way it did, then you're living in the past. People are right about not living in the past. The past is over! Don't look back and move on to what's next. But your family should never be in your past; they're your family. For parents who've left their kids behind. Be in your kids life, your kids need that! It's never too late to make a change!

Of coarse rich people will be upset reading this because they donate the most amount of money to charity. The rich do donate a lot to church and to good causes. I'd have to say that they donate just enough not to make themselves uncomfortable in their lifestyle. I have met people who donate a lot, but I have never met the person who donated it all. I'm not saying I would, but I'm also not the person telling you what book to follow. Even though it's for a good cause. I almost see it as taking money from the people who work for you and giving it to others. I think giving makes people feel better about themselves and justifies, for them, keeping the remainder of what they have. People always say when they're poor that if they become rich, they will help other poor people out. Most of the time as people make more money, they spend more money. Because they believe they have worked hard and earned it. So don't sit around and wait for some rich person to help you out, it just ain't gonna happen. I'll defiantly admit that letting go of your money is hard to do! Some rich people believe shopping is the same as giving money to charity. This is not true! Or that they're doing a good thing by shopping cause they're stimulating the economy, maybe? It's still ultimately a system where the poor serve the rich. Where the rich take advantage of the poor, and the educated take advantage of the uneducated.

For those of you who don't know the Bible as well as others, here are some of the verses I base my views on. "It's easier for a camel to go though the eye of a needle then for a rich man to enter the kingdom of heaven." Matthew 19:24. "Blessed are the meek, for they shall inherit the earth." Matthew 5:5. Jesus told one man to sell everything he had, give it to the poor, and follow him. Of course people will explain these verses differently. We all read the Bible differently. The Bible does talk about you being blessed 30, 60, 100 times of what you give. Again this is outside of the gospels. I believe the words of Jesus would have to supercede the rest.

I don't have all the solutions for helping the poor. Seems like anybody I ever tried to help ended up screwing me. I guess if you give, you have to do it with the intention of not getting anything in return.

Religious people usually don't like scientists' views on things because it's usually not the same views as the Religious sector. But a religious person doesn't hesitate to use a microwave or cell phone. Which were brought to us by Science. Currently the evidence in Physics is telling us that we don't live in a universe but a multiverse. Meaning there's a possibility that there are an infinite number of other universes. Which also means there could be other Earth's or even copies of you and me. That there are eleven dimensions, seven past the ones we can see. These theories do not prove or disprove the existence of God. Maybe God made things so massively large and infinitely small so we could never figure it out? Einstein's theories on time show that time speeds up and slows down, depending on your movement. We never move fast enough to see its effects. But it shows that past, present, and future all exist somewhere.

From a biblical view, it's hard to believe that dinosaurs existed at the same time as man.

The Bible mentions something in the book of Job that could be described as a dinosaur. I guess the biblical view is that dinosaurs died during the great flood? It's hard to imagine dinosaurs being on Noah's ark. Of course Science says dinosaurs died over 65 million years ago. I'd heard both views that support evolution and that debunk it. Humans have changed their average height just over the last few hundred years, showing some form of evolution does happen. Then again, something like your eye cannot evolve. It has so many working parts that if just one part wasn't there, then your eye wouldn't work.

Another view on the stories of the Bible is that; all the accounts of when people talked to angels or when God came down from the sky, that is was actually aliens that came from another planet. I know most people would immediately dismiss that but you have to ask yourself some questions. Why were there so many pyramid structures built around the world, with the cultures having no way of knowing each other? Structures astronomically aligned, and so perfectly built that we can't duplicate many of these structures today. Why were the ancients so focused on astronomy? Most of the ancient stories handed down are mythological. What if the ancients were telling the truth of what they saw? There are more stars in the sky then there are grains of sand on Earth. It's pretty much a mathematical certainty there is another Earthlike planet out there somewhere. One truth, as time goes along, is that Religion changes its views as Science discovers more and more. 500 years ago if you said the Earth was round, you could have been put to death. Or if you said the Earth isn't the center of the solar system.

The Old Testament is a lot more brutal in its laws where the New Testament is more of a loving nature. Of course everybody knows the Ten Commandments in the Old Testament but the Old Testament also talks about an eye for an eye, if you rape a virgin she must marry you, how it's ok to own slaves and how to treat and beat them. Why couldn't the Bible just say that slavery is wrong? You can lay some of the blame for slavery on these things being in the Bible. Because most people take their pastor's interpretation of the Bible over their own. A pastor has a considerable amount of power! They hold people's greatest hopes in the palm of their hands. Because people themselves don't have all the answers, and they think this person does. That's why the Bible can be as much harmful as it can be helpful. All that depends on what agenda the pastor wants to push.

Most people just go to church to be part of a social scene, like an extension of high school. Its funny how the church wants everybody to volunteer their time but the pastor gets paid for his/hers. A lot of people look at church like, I'll just continue to do what I want then ask for forgiveness. That's one reason it's hard for me to take it serious when others don't. It's not that hard to do what's right, or know what's right. But people think I'll just tell this one more lie or go out and drink, and ask for forgiveness the next day. I see a lot though Religion that your life sucks now or you have a crappy job but just keep doing it and when you die, you'll have everything then. And this makes the person happy when really nothing changed. You're still working the crappy job. And how does this person know you'll have everything when you die? Has he or she been there?

This is probably why so many people get mistreated at work. Cause the Christian boss or owner sees the slavery viewpoint of the Bible, and looks at their employees as slaves. And since it was God approved in the Old Testament and not specifically condemned in the New Testament, they think they are doing God's will. All I can do is think about this and shake my head! Slavery ended after the Civil War but it really didn't end until the 1950's and 1960's cause of sharecropping and peonage, practices that were slavery under a different name. Then in the 1970's we began our global trade policies. Which are sweatshops making a lot of our products. So did we really end slavery or just outsource it?

A lot of churches you go into are full of old people. There are a couple of reasons for this. One, they're old and they're getting close to death or the unknown. Two, they probably have nothing better to do. Some people when they get close to death, want to tell other people how to live a better life. They do this to try and makeup for all the bad things they've done in their own lives. I'd just try to ignore these people and be young. Enjoy life before it passes you by.

My goal here isn't to talk anyone out of a Religion. It's to warn a person on the outside not to expect all people of faith to practice what they preach. I was pretty shocked of this entering the work world. How the work world is so different from the church world even though they involve the same people. It just seems to me that people follow faith on a "best effort" basis. Which isn't against what Religion teaches, it just wasn't what I expected.

Chapter 3: Relationships

I pray that everybody finds true love in life! I do believe it exists. It's just a lot more rare than I thought before. I hate to say this but most women marry for money/security and/or looks. And most men marry for looks and/or character quality of the women. Women who marry for money are basically legal prostitutes. Which made me think if that's the case, we might as well have legalized prostitution. But women don't want this, that would take away their monopoly or power. The number one thing couples fight about is money, that's a fact. I'm glad women have their own equal rights; I would if I were a women. That's probably why the divorce rate is so much higher now. Cause women don't have to put up with their husbands crap anymore. Back in the old days, men basically own their women like property. Which was good for the men but not the women.

So pick your spouse carefully, take your time! Don't rush into a marriage. Marriage is a very big step! Do it when you and your spouse think it's the right time. I definitely don't believe in no sex before marriage. Cause people will just rush out and get married just to have sex. Now having said that, let me also say. If you're going to have sex, use protection! A baby is the biggest and longest thing that will change your life! You don't need to have a kid from some guy you don't know. A kid doesn't need to grow up like that! A kid needs to grow up around a good stable family. I don't believe in abortion either, unless medically necessary. Abortion is no different than murder to me. If you kill a baby right before it's born, it's an abortion. Right after birth it's murder. Now I know abortion laws have changed over the years. An abortion, in many states, has to take place within the first twelve weeks. From a law point of view, the Constitution states you have the right to LIFE, Liberty, and the pursuit of happiness. It doesn't say you have the right to death.

Sex isn't just some non-event that everybody does. It's a very big deal! Things can result from sex that you can't even imagine now. You think a guy loves you, you get pregnant, and he's gone. A girl gets pregnant and is going to have an abortion against your will. And if you're the guy willing to take care of the kid you always wanted. She has the abortion anyway and you have to live with that for the rest of your life! Or you have one wild night and then you get herpes, or some other STD for the rest of your life! These are things that can't be changed after the fact. So think carefully before you act! And men; if you're willing to have sex, TAKE RESPONSIBILITY FOR YOUR ACTIONS! TAKE CARE OF YOUR KIDS! Too many kids running around out here without a dad! And women, try to make things work also!

As far as people dating, people are always waiting for Mr. or Ms. right to come in their life. Again going back to some magical force. Relationships are tricky cause different people are looking for different things. One person may be looking for the right person to spend the rest of their life with, while the other is just looking for a good time. The problem is that people constantly lie to each other, tell the other person what they want to hear just to get what THEY want. The human race is really a self-centered selfish group of beings. People ultimately only care about themselves. Which really makes sense as every person's life is their own, but nobody will ever tell you this.

Love is a game, just like everything else in life. You have to know the rules of the game and how to play it. I see a guy who wonders why he can't get a girlfriend. Wonders when that "magical force" will send a girl in his life. When in reality, he should do one or more of the following things; get pumped up in the gym, get a high paying job, increase his looks, work in management, or lower his standards. The same goes for girls in this same situation. I feel sorry for people like this! Because they've been told life is a certain way that it's not, and it's where church can suck people in. A nerdy looking guy praying that God will send him a girlfriend or vice versa. When really it goes back to the laws of supply and demand. I say this because you never or hardly see a fat jobless guy with a Playboy bunny girl. If love was really what's on the inside of a person, this would happen. Now I'm not saying I don't believe in true love or destiny. I'm just saying you have to live in reality also. People tell these ugly people that things will happen, just wait. Because the person is just being nice, or to me lying if they're not saying what's really on their mind. When I think this person could really be hurting this single person instead of telling them what they really need to hear.

You don't see this happen when somebody needs a job. You don't hear somebody say, "just wait, it will happen." No, when it comes to work you hear the truth! When it comes to a job the person will say, "Are you looking hard enough? Maybe you need to go back to school." Funny how you have the same situation with love and employment, and you get two different answers. When people look for what they want in another person. They act no different than what you see on the animal channel. A female peacock picks the male peacock with the prettiest feathers or who does the best dance. Or two rams butt heads until one gives up and the other gets the female ram. You'll notice this same behavior between men and women in everyday life. Maybe us humans get this through our evolution?

If you are looking for your "soulmate." I hope you find him/her! I am sorry of all the crap, games, lies, heartache, etc, you have to go through to find that person.

Now on the subject of kids, don't have kids until YOU know you are ready! Don't have kids until YOU know you're ready! DON'T HAVE KIDS UNTIL YOU KNOW YOU ARE READY! Okay, so now I have your attention on that. Kids are such a blessing and are the greatest joy of life, but I'm screaming this to you cause they will change your life FOREVER.

Kids are not something you get to play with for a few hours and take them back to the store. They are yours 24 hours a day, seven days a week. It never ends, and no matter what age they are, you always worry about them. Before you have kids, you're free to do what YOU want to do. If you want to travel two states away on a spare of the moment, you can. If you want to go live somewhere else for a time, you can do that also, and that all ends when you have kids. Kids can't ride in a car for a long time. If you stay in a car too long, they'll take a nap and throw their sleep off schedule. It takes forever to get out of the house and once you finally do, they crap all over themselves. You don't get good sleep anymore cause they either cough or kick you all night, but it is all worth it!!

The point I'm trying to make is; whatever you wanted to do in life, do it before you have kids. Things like going to Hawaii, traveling, hobbies, parties, etc. If you're going to college, working, and don't think you have any time, you're wrong! You'll realize that when you have kids. You have all the time in the world before having kids. Kids get easier as they get older. They'll get their own friends, and won't want to have anything to do with mom and dad anymore. That is also sad! The little babies you raised 24 hours a day from birth don't want to spend time with you, but that's just part of life. Kids realize these things once they have kids of their own. Do you see how life gets more complicated the older you get? The things that made you happy when you were younger don't as you get older, and vice versa. When I was younger, it would have been my dream to be the biggest richest rock star on the planet. If that happened to me now, I'd be playing in front of millions of fans, making millions of dollars, and the envy of everyone. Even then I wouldn't be the happiest person, cause I'd have to do so while missing my kids. They change your whole outlook on life!

When it comes to government, I believe the government should stay out of your life as much as possible. I would have to make one exception to that, maybe? Think about how many unwanted, unplanned babies are born. Since I don't believe in abortion, I thought of my best alternative. What if the government gave every male a vasectomy at age 17, which is reversible? The vasectomy would be free, paid for by the government. When you, and your partner, decide you're ready to have kids. You pay to have the vasectomy reversed, not to exceed a cost of $300. That would show these people are ready to have kids and would take good care of them. Then all the other people who just care to have sex, can do just that. Just an idea I had to make sure every kid has loving guardians.

This reminds me of something else. It's a trend right now for American families to adopt kids from third world countries. These people think they are making the world a better place, one kid at a time. How do you not know if these kids were kidnapped by child protective services of that government, sold, and the government makes all the money from the adoption? To most people that would sound far fetched, but you never know what really goes on. You think you could be helping somebody when you really could be hurting them. I wonder this because I trust no one, nothing I read or see, what I'm told, just what happens in my everyday life.

Everybody always has an agenda to what they're doing. I try to think for myself, and figure out what makes the most sense to me based on everyday life! Sometimes in life you'll notice the people who give you a solution were also the ones who caused the problem. There were rumors before that the people who made software to fix virus's on your computer, were also the same people who release the virus in the first place so you'll buy their products. Don't know if that's true or not? Sounds possible and nothing would surprise me. I think a lot more scenario's like this happen more than we think they do.

  As far as friendships in your life; Just know about 90% of your friends are only there cause you can do something for them, or that they might need something from you one day in the future. The second you can't do anything for anybody is when you'll lose all your friends. I always thought the friends I made would be there for life in some sense, but you can't live in the past cause it's already over. People that live in the past can never see the future. You can't depend on anybody being there in your future cause life is always changing. People I have seen everyday for years, that I thought would always be there, are gone. So all you really have is this present moment, right now. That's all you really own in life, is today. So make the most out of each moment! Life is way too short to be unhappy about anything. If you are unhappy for too many days, then you need to change something. I've learned that you can't really expect anything out of people for things you have done for them. It just doesn't work that way.

Which in turn has made me not want to do anything for others. Of course if there's some poor kid starving I'd help him or her, but I've been screwed over too many times by all types of people. You want to help others; it makes you feel good that you made a difference! But more than not, people just take advantage of you!

People have always expected a lot out of me. Wanted me to be there for them. But when the table was turned, they could care less about me. People really only care about what they want to do in the moment. Guess you can call that selfish, or call it being human. People hardly ever think about the other person and put the shoe on the other foot. I know I've screwed some people over in my past, but I didn't think about it as much as when it happened to me. The people who stick around when you have nothing are your real friends. A true friend is one who breaks and then stays for the mend. You should tell these people how thankful you are for having them!

You've heard, "treat others how you would like to be treated." This is just more crap too. Again, excluding your family. I'd rephrase it to," treat others how they treat you." Cause if you did the first, people would never learn any lessons of how crappy they are. This also makes you stand your ground. You got to stand up for yourself in life. Cause if you don't, people will always run over you! A lot like the animal kingdom. Animals have to kill something everyday in order to eat. You can really learn a lot from watching nature. I am thankful that if I ever do make it big. I'll know the real reason why people will want to be around me.

If you have problems finding a date, take a hard look at yourself in the mirror and see what you could improve on. It always seems easier to find faults in other people beside yourself. First impressions do matter! You probably judge a person in the first 10 seconds you meet him, and the same is done to you. The best place to meet people are places you go to on a regular basis, work, church, school, etc. of course this is increasingly changing with online social sites.

Don't think that being nice will get you anywhere. Just like the saying, "nice guys finish last." This is a world that is ruled by force. Nothing is given to you; you must take it from somebody else. Not talking about stealing, talking in a sense of the whole pie.

It's a good and noble cause to take care of old people. It's one thing to do it as a job or as a fraction of your time, but it wouldn't be something I'd do 24 hours a day. A lot of people feel sorry for people in retirement homes, and I do too. But I would also have to live my life also. Remember when these people were young; there were old people in retirement homes too. They were out partying, working, living life while their elders were in retirement homes. It's just the cycle of life. When I'm in a retirement home one day, I'll be lonely too. But I wouldn't expect a young person to spend 24 hours a day with me while they miss out on their own life. It sucks, but that's just the way it is. Young people want to get out and experience the world while they can, and I don't blame them.

Now middle-aged people who want to do everything for their grown kids like grocery shop, buy them stuff, give them money, etc. You might as well let them. They probably have nothing better to do with their lives, that's why they want to do so much for their grown kids. It also makes them feel good. Plus at the same time, society doesn't always reward people who make it on their own. Most people get ahead by who their parents are. Some people want to be independent and do everything on their own. I just look at it like if the person offers, take advantage of it. But also don't let the same people act like you owe them something just because they did something for you, when you didn't ask for it.

Chapter 4: Work

Work is probably the largest part of our lives. When you're a kid, you do whatever your parents tell you to do cause they are your life support. Then when you go to work, work is your life support. So you basically have to do whatever your job tells you to do. So you have owners, somebody owns you. Now is work freedom or slavery? Guess that is debatable. I'd say if you do what you love, don't depend on others, and are happy. I'd say that's freedom. If you go to work everyday, absolutely hate it, and have no way of bettering yourself. I'd call that a very light form of economic slavery. I used the term slavery very carefully cause those people had no rights, freedom, got beat, worked all the time, and died. So don't think I'm trying to say an 1800's slave is the same as a minimum wage worker. I'm Just trying to say what is real freedom in the workplace.

Everybody says they either want to own their own business or just work for somebody but in reality everybody owns their own business, whether you have an employer or not. I say this because you have to do a good job at your current job, so you'll get a good reference when you leave to go to the next job. You really don't ever just work a job. Your job is your business. If you are a secretary, then secretarial is your business. If you cook hamburgers, then hamburgers are your business.

There really is no job security like there was 50 years ago. People back then got a job, and stayed there the rest of their lives. Today the average person stays at a job 4-5 years.

When I was younger, I didn't know getting a good job was so hard. I just thought you signed some papers and got your paycheck because everybody has bills they have to pay. That's just not how it works. All business cares about is making money, that's it! They need people to do work cause the owner can't do it all, and you need a job to pay your bills.

That's where supply and demand come in effect. Chances are the employer can replace you faster than you can find another job. This gives the employer an edge over you in the game. Just like here in America, employers were having a hard time filling low paying jobs in the last 10-20 years. So according to supply and demand, they needed to offer more money to attract workers. Instead, the government allows illegal aliens to illegally come over and fill the jobs. This shows where the government, including both political parties, is on the side of money and business. Not the common person.

You have market value to your labor. You're paid for a job compared to what someone else will do it for. People don't really notice it but the power is really in the collective.

I think the common person got too powerful when unions were commonplace. I think global free trade was the business elites solution for getting rid of unions. Allowing companies to go overseas and import goods back home. The people overseas make around $1 per hour, while the same job here will pay $15 per hour. We will never be able to compete with that! Unless our pay goes down, their pay goes up, or a combination of the two. Today's work world is more of a "good old boy" network. In many cases it probably comes down to more of who you know, then what you know. Employers like to hire friends or family of employees cause they want to know as much as they can about someone they're hiring. Many of the things we have in work today come from unions. You can thank vacation time, benefits, holiday pay, safe working conditions, fair treatment, etc., to unions. I think another reason the elite don't like unions are because unions base work on seniority, and the elite don't want their son or daughter to have to start at the bottom like everybody else. A lot of people like to bash on unions or that they're bad for our way of life. Having a union is no less capitalistic than a non-union workplace. Either way is free market capitalism at work.

Culture tries to brainwash you in saying to make it in America, it's all on merit. Hearing this growing up this made me believe employers line up all the resumes and hire the person with the best skills, and that everybody moves up at work fairly through their seniority. This is not true. An employer either hires a buddy or a person who they think is the best all around for the job. A college education doesn't matter to an employer as much as being licensed to do a job or your work experience. If you have a college degree and are not licensed in something. An employer doesn't necessarily have to fill the job you're applying for with a college-educated person. They could even hire an uneducated foreigner over you if they wanted to. If an employer has to fill a job with a licensed person, then he or she can't just give that job to a buddy. It has to be a licensed person. That's where your license becomes more valuable then a lot of college degrees. Employers care more about work experience then college degrees, but it's better to have both. Just don't expect to get a good high-paying job right out of college. You have to start at the bottom and work your way up.

Employers like to give jobs to people they like. So if the boss is drinking, he's going to like whoever's drinking with him. Your attitude and likeability are just as much, if not more important, than what degree you have when concerning work. That to is sad and people are supposed to judge you on your actions, not your words. But in reality, it's just the opposite. People are so easily bullshitted! People get lied to over and over again by the same person, and yet the person always believes them. Like something has changed. This just shows how stupid and gullible people really are.

People try to explain the work world as whoever does the hardest work and the best job gets moved up. This isn't totally true either. It gives the impression that if you have a hard working 18 year old and a lazy 40 year old and a management position comes available, that the 18 year old would get the job on merit. Just isn't true, unless the 18 year old is the owner's child. A company isn't going to put an 18 year old in charge over middle-aged people. It would piss the middle-aged people off. Companies also like to put people who are big and strong, we'll call them jocks, in management positions. That way to physically intimidate the other workers. So that's another strike against you smaller people. So if you're a young worker, don't work too hard and enjoy being young! You have the rest of your life to work. Chances are you're not going to be real successful until later in life. Upper management likes to tell the young workers that, :If you work real hard and do everything I tell you to do, you'll be a manager in a couple of years." This makes the young worker happy. When in reality nothing real happened, just empty words. Then time goes by, nothing happens, and they hire people off the street in positions higher than you. So try not to give your job your life, and enjoy being young. Cause you're only young once!

So how did the rich person get rich? Did they work an entry-level job, save their hard earned money over many years, then go start their business? No, most of them go and get a business loan from a bank. The bank probably doesn't have the money either, so they make it up though a promissory note. Then if the business fails, if set up right, the bankruptcy can't come back of their personal home or assets. They just won't be able to get another business loan for a while. So they don't follow the advice they give their employees about doing the right thing, working hard, and slowly moving their way up. Sounds like a pretty sweet deal to me!

Some people joke about how wealthy people are just very good con artist. Who knows, could be true? I pretty much view everybody as trying to sell me something. That they'll put all their values aside until the sale is over and then ask for forgiveness. Work is basically a pyramid scheme. If you draw the employees from the CEO down, you'd have a pyramid. Except the con here isn't money, its work. And the pay results in a reversed pyramid. Managers and Business owners have a stereotype of being greedy assholes. This could be true. But in their defense, you have to be somewhat of an asshole as a manager.

Or people will run over you, it just comes with the territory.

Half of the degrees that colleges offer are a waste of time and money. Degrees in teaching, healthcare, legal, etc, are the better degrees that will get you a job. Degrees in art, radio, music, history, etc., not necessarily. A lot of those degrees you can learn without going to college. I thought just having a degree; I'd be better off than most people. That simply isn't true. You have to know how to do something specific, that there is a need for, or know a lot of people! Employers do not want to spend their money to train you. This is where people with work experience have an advantage.

If you're lucky to land a middle-class job, you'll probably always just be getting by. The big money doesn't come unless you, own your own business, work in commission, or have a rare high demand skill.

A lot of people who didn't like high school couldn't wait for it to be over. I hate to tell you that high school never really ends. People all through life act like they did in high school.

They care what other people think about them, buckle to peer pressure, follow the crowd, screw over whoever it takes to be accepted, hang out with people according to social status, etc. People even act like this in their 60s, how sad! I was amazed of how many people never grow up. The real world looks a lot like the high school world. The jocks and hot chicks run the high school, the same goes for the real world. Not all the time, but a lot. The jocks are the business owners and managers, and the hot chicks don't work. Since they're hot, they go shopping all day.

Culture tells you that anybody can make it in America if you work hard enough. Which for the most part is true but what you're not told is that half, if not more, of all people get their jobs cause of their parents or from somebody they know. Well then how is that based on merit? So one person works their ass off, goes to college, and gets a job. While another person just signs a form cause of who his/her parents are. Not saying I wouldn't do the same for my kids, it's just something never talked about. Just like in school where certain kids get on the basketball or football team cause of how big of a donation their parents made to the school. The real world is no different. You don't notice these things as much at the time. You thought everybody tried out and people got on the team based on their skills. A lot did but some didn't. Like they say, "if you have enough money, you can buy anything." That is one advantage to owning your own business, that you can give your job to your kid. You can't do that if you're an employee.

Remember when working or looking for a job, you are your name. What do you think people think of when they hear your name? Pretty powerful isn't it?

Employers want you to do what ever it takes. Work any time they need you to work. Help any way you can when people call out or work overtime when business is heavy, and any other favors you can think of. But the second your employer doesn't have a need for you anymore you're let go, nice how that works. When business was booming did the employers give extra money to its workers? Not much, most of the money is used to expand the business. But when hard times hit people are let go. It's a double win for the business.

I wonder how a major corporation that does 10 times the business as their competitor pays the same pay as the competitor. This just shows that even if your company makes a lot of money, it doesn't mean you will. You will just be paid your market value. This further shows that things are up to you! Nobodies going to do anything for you other than maybe your parents.

There is no point in fighting with your job. You can't change what other people think. Don't try to play revenge with people at work and get them back. You're only hurting yourself! It's better to just smile and move on with your life. Go work somewhere, where you are respected! You can't hurt your employer. They have the upper hand over you. You can be replaced at any job you do at any time. Just accept you have an owner, do a good job, get a paycheck, and go home. Go with your heart and your intuitions in life. Some how they know where you should go even when others don't. If something sucks for too long, then change it.

I always thought that working a job again, was based on merit, basically how much work you do and how good of a job you do. I've found that to be only about half of it. The other half is how good of an ass kisser you are. Something I've never been good at. So whoever degrades themselves the most, doesn't have a brain of their own, has a company mentality not an individual one, and acts like a slave gets promoted. Pretty nice isn't it?

People always think that if they do things the "right way," that they will be better off than the person who is a piece of crap. I've come to find that these two people are not that different. One person works his ass off and never gets anywhere. While the other person does what he wants and always somehow manages. A lot of people just believe life has to be hard and just accept it. They believe all the people having fun and doing wrong will someday pay for it. Some do with drug overdoses and accidental pregnancies, but you also have to somewhat enjoy yourself also. It seems that the people who take chances and do what they love, get the reward. While the people who play it safe, work hard their whole life have nothing.

Real wealth isn't if you have a TV, a nice car, or a big house. To me, real wealth is measured in what you own without debt and your happiness. One person can have nothing and be happy. That's richness to me. While another person can have everything material but isn't happy. Which this is poorness to me. Happiness is really just a state of mind. We're past the point of getting what we need to survive on a daily basis in America. A majority are really just things we want. We could one day in America worry if we'll survive the next day, but that day isn't today.

You would think the people who do the hard physical work would make the big money, and the others would make less money. But it's just the opposite. Just doesn't make sense. I know it has to do with skill level and supply/demand economics. I am not saying a doctor should make the same as a person who cooks hamburgers. But a person who cooks hamburgers should still make a decent wage because they are still doing work. And there are a lot of people who make as much as a doctor and didn't work very hard to get there doing a desk job.

I ran across a friend one day and we were talking about a wealthy individual. I said he was probably at the country club again playing golf, jokingly. His reply was, "well, he earned it." That started to make me think. Yeah this person has worked his whole life and got ahead. He now has the time and money to enjoy himself. Then I thought about the 60-year-old who has flipped hamburgers his whole life. What has he earned? They both work there 40 hours a week. I know one job has a higher skill level than the other, but they're also both working. All the guy flipping hamburgers apparently has earned is another day of work. Now of course the guy flipping hamburgers probably didn't have to stay in that job his whole life, but maybe he did? Maybe it was the only job he could get? But if the guy flipping hamburgers takes a day off, that's wrong. The country club guy looks down on the hamburger guy when he takes a day off. He thinks the hamburger guy should be at work, but he doesn't think he himself has to work cause he earned it.

It's mind boggling for me to think of the difference in income of people. You have one person who makes millions, is his/her own boss, has their own office with personal bathroom and kitchen, owns everything they have without debt, pays people to fix anything that breaks, drinks alcohol on the clock if they want, gets a large severance when let go, everybody worships the ground they walk on, and they set their own hours. While another makes minimum wage, works whatever hours they're told to, does work outside of work (like mow grass, cook, clean, house upkeep, car maintenance, etc.), might get unemployment when let go, has very little benefits, every person they work with is their boss, gets no respect, and owns nothing. It's one class of people who serve another. The rich make all the money, manage, and own everything. The poor and middle class do all the work.

People say you spend all your health though life on working, and the last two years of your life you spend all of your wealth back on your health. For all of you workaholics, at what point do you just sit back and enjoy God's creation? Now if you love to work, by all means do it! People always say how they love to work and work is good for you. I don't see how work is good if the second you get health problems from working; your employer lets you go. Hard work is good in the sense if you do what you love. It's sad when people have kids and neither parent wants to quit their job to take care of them, somewhat to do out of greed. Then the kids get dropped off at daycare all the time, and daycare is the one raising your kids. These parents are giving up time they'll never get back. Then what did you have kids for?

I don't think the person on their deathbed wishes they could go back and work some more. I'm sure in most cases they wish they had spent more time with family. Hard work pays off? Hard work doesn't pay the same for everybody. Hard work pays off for the country club guy, not the hamburger guy.

I started working at the age of 15. At that point I paid all my expenses except rent and health insurance. I started paying rent when I moved out. So I worked while going to college, graduated, and continued working. My average cohort might have got a part-time job in high school. If they did, it was spending money for them. They didn't have to pay any bills, got a car, moved off to college, might or might not of paid for it, partied while at college, graduated maybe, and for most got their first job at 25. I had ten years work experience over this person, and they get more pay and a better job than me. Where did hard work pay off here? How was I better off doing things the "right way?" Some would argue that working at that age keeps you out of trouble or makes you learn the value of a dollar. I guess some of that could be true. I know I missed out on some fun times I'll never get back, but that's life. You do the best with what you have! I know this sounds like a pity party, I'm just telling you this to show how what you hear or see is not always true.

Another example is that my wife could have had her entire college paid for by the government, given her situation. Instead she worked and paid her own college. She saved the government lots of money. I thought it was the right thing to do at the time. But how is she any better off going through that entire struggle? I'm sure the grants she turned down were just given to somebody else anyways. It was frustrating to work and pay for college while everybody else didn't work, went for free, and got the good jobs. Makes you feel like a sucker! It would've paid off for us if we had got better degrees.

People always complain about other people living off welfare, and rightly so. The government has made it in such a way, that unless you have a really good job, the welfare person and the average worker make about the same money. That makes you think, what's the incentive for going to work? I think government expands welfare, because they want to be able to control your life. One difference here is the welfare person becomes a dependent person, then not being able to do anything on his or her own. The welfare system distorts the free market. The more people that get on food stamps, the higher it makes the price of food for everybody else. The more people that get free college or college loans, drives the price of college up for everybody because of supply/demand economics. So do these programs really help? There are people who need these programs but the majority of these people are able-bodied, just getting something for free. The person, who loses the most in this, is the one who works at a low-wage job and doesn't get any of the programs.

I know that I've bashed rich people a lot on here. Really in reality all people are equally shitty. The only difference is that some have more money than others. Everything is a lie, everybody has his or her own agenda, and almost nothing is real. You can work around middle and lower class people and they'll tell on you just the same. I've seen people spend half their workday in the office telling on others of how other people don't work. I'm sitting there thinking, while I'm working, how much work could this person be doing if they're in the office all day? But managers like people like this, cause it's less managing they have to do! Whatever happened when you were in school, you were told to mine your own business and to not tell on others? Well, that becomes rewarded and encouraged later in life. Work is about like a reality show. People get together and see who they are going to vote off that week. People always think it's funny when somebody loses their job, gets a divorce, or whatever etc., until it happens to them. That says something about humans. You pretty much have to view yourself as being better than everybody else to be successful. People are competitive all though life from birth to death. From look how big my house is to look at what car I drive. I don't guess it's wrong to show off what you've worked for but it also shouldn't consume you either.

When it comes to work anybody will throw you under the bus to save their own job. Even your best friends, family, etc. People lose their values when it comes to their job. These same people will talk to you after work like nothing happened. It's just considered business. So try not to have very high expectations out of the people you work with!

Christians are always trying to get more people to join their cause of following the Bible. That they're always trying to combat the "Non-Believers." Maybe it would help if they put their money where their mouth is and promote people at work based on how Christian they are. The more you lead a Christian life, the more you advance and when you sin you move down the career ladder. This would give people the incentive to lead a better life. I know this isn't practical, I'm just making a point. I always love when a boss says, "we all work together as a team!" But we never get paid like a team, one person gets paid more than another.

Chapter 5: Government

The world wouldn't be a very nice place if we didn't have government. Which should also say something about humankind; we are not designed to get along with each other. Governments can be oppressive and are not perfect either. Through history, man has discovered that representative government is the best form. Not any one person can have too much power. There is a saying that absolute power corrupts absolutely. We are not a democracy in America. America is a representative republic. Some argue the world has gone more toward fascism ever since WWII.

People always want to believe somebody is watching out for them and their well being. That somebody in government will fix their lives. This for the most part isn't true. You are on your own, and government shouldn't be there for everything in your life. The government's first priority should be to protect your freedom and the rule of law.

Both parties run on campaigns saying they are going to fix everything that is broken. But if they did that, you wouldn't need politicians anymore. So they set up government in a way so you'll need them. Both parties are just a mirage to give you the perception of a choice. When really these things are already planned behind closed doors. When you look at it; Democrats hate business and love government, and Republicans hate government and love business. That way they keep everybody fighting with each other while they go off, eat dinner, and party. There's a lot of talk of social warfare, how poor people shouldn't be jealous of rich people. But when rich and middle class people get mad at a poor person living off the government, isn't that also social warfare? And why is it when poor people get money from the government its called welfare, but when rich people get money from the government its called a bailout?

Government, like everything else, is controlled by money. I believe there are people who are more powerful than the politicians, the financiers. Think about it, if I give five dollars to a campaign and somebody else gives a million. Who is the politician going to listen to? You can buy anything if you have enough money. All the financier has to say is, "vote for plan A or you don't get any money for your next campaign." The real power is in numbers, groups of people. People can change anything if you have enough of a crowd to do it, but the majority of people are too busy with everyday life. This is the way the government wants it. So if you're conservative, vote conservative. If you're a liberal, vote liberal. Just try not to get too wrapped up in the game. Your life is too short to wrap up too much time in something that isn't going to change. The sad truth about history is that people don't pay attention until something bad happens. As long as times are good, people don't care about anything important.

I highly respect our military for the job they

do! I have never served. Thought about it when I was younger, but wanted to go to college instead. My thoughts on military service have changed over the years. Because I don't 100% believe everything I see or hear on the news. For example, because this country attacked us, we have to go retaliate. How do I know this really happened? I wasn't there. How do you not know if government has an agenda to do something and they caused the problem? When 9/11 happened, people acted like we had never been attacked before. It was a surprise to them but not as much to me, cause I've read history. It amazes me how people's history only goes back to when they were born. Like nothing happened before that. I think it's wrong to get mad at any person who questions anything about our country. It's not unpatriotic to have a dissenting view, just the opposite. You should go wherever the evidence leads you!

I watched a program a while back on WWII. The European countries our military freed had a ceremony to thank them for their service. I thought that's nice. Risk your life and get thanked. I thought, couldn't these countries pass a tax on the freed citizens and give it to the servicemen who freed them? Some people argue that the people you're fighting for put the people you're fighting against, in power. If that were true, that's something I couldn't fight for. The point of life is survival.

When I think of war, I try to think if it would be something I would send my own kids to. People are quick to say we need to go to war but wouldn't fight it themselves. It's a good thing we have a voluntary force! Here's one way I look at war; middle-class and poor are sent off to war. The wealthy kids are left back home with all the women. The politicians care about the cause but most not enough to send their own kids. Then the ones who survive come back home. Some have a hard time getting a job, fitting back into society, or are years behind in their lives. We just don't do enough for our military. I guess war means something different to everybody depending on how they view the enemy. Whether they believe it's a real one or a made-up one. A good number of people believe there should be a reduction in the world's population. How do you not know that war isn't a way to achieve this? A lot of the dictators we overthrow, are the ones we put in power. I just hope that our leaders are doing things in America's best interest! I guess that's a leap of faith I'll have to take. I just hate to see people get hard-core into anything. Whether it's a political party, politician, religion, family, friends, preachers, etc. Cause these people always fall short of your expectations. When you go hard-core, you put your trust in these people so much that you'll defend them even when they're wrong. And when you do that, you're no better than the people you're arguing against. I've been guilty of it too. You have to stay true to yourself and just make the best choices you can. How do you know the things that you watch on the news are real? How do you know when you're shown a video of the enemy, that's real? How do you know it wasn't made in a studio somewhere? You don't. The only reason you believe it's real is because you don't think people are that dishonest. That, that many people could be involved in a lie. The news is made up for an agenda, just like any sitcom. Maybe not as much made up as being selective of what stories are talked about. It's called propaganda; it used the time all over the world.

Chapter 6:
Taxes and Money

Taxes will probably be the largest expense in your life. By the time you add up income tax, property tax, sales tax, phone tax, cable tax, vacation tax, car tax, Internet tax, business tax, and any other taxes or fees. A lot of the taxes you pay are hidden. Like business taxes or tax through inflation. When businesses have to pay tax, they role it into the cost of doing business. Business is in business to make a profit, not to pay taxes. You pay these costs when you buy a product. Inflation happens when government prints money that isn't backed by any hard asset like gold, silver, property, etc. For example; if inflation is at 5%, that's really you paying a 5% tax. Because your money doesn't buy what it did the previous year. Inflation also happens when banks loan money they don't have, usually called credit. Every time you use your credit card, you're expanding the money supply. And every time you pay your credit card off, you're contracting it. Inflation is a hidden tax, and governments love using it cause most people don't know they're paying it.

If I had to choose one form of taxation, it would be a sales tax. Because sales tax is the same percentage for everybody and everybody pays it. Even drug dealers, tax cheats, etc., would pay the tax. The tax system we currently have picks and chooses who pays it. The people who get around this are the smart educated professionals. Which again disenfranchises the uneducated poor. Our tax system is a redistribution of wealth. Which give rich people the position to say they take care of the poor. Which I look at it like; if the poor didn't get an income tax check from the government, they would make more money at their jobs cause of supply/demand economics.

Rich people say they pay all the taxes. On paper they do but to me in theory, they pay no more than anybody else. First of all, rich people pay all the taxes but the middle and poor do all the hard physical work. The jobs nobody wants. Second; if a business passes its tax cost down to the consumer, (in reality it's the consumer paying the business tax, not the business), then how come that same principle doesn't apply to income taxes? People, rich or poor, factor in their income tax cost into their price of labor as a collective according to supply/demand economics. For example, if you put a tax on plumbers, they'll raise their prices to cover the new tax. So the consumer is paying the tax, not the plumbers. This is how rich people pay no more tax than anybody else. They factor in their tax cost into their price of labor as a collective. This accomplishes many things. It makes the middle and poor classes feel like they pay little or no income taxes. It puts rich people in the position that they have helped the poor. It makes the poor and middle classes dependent on government. It makes government look like a savior by giving rebate checks. Even though poor people don't pay taxes. The tax they pay is the work they do. Governments, no matter if they're capitalistic or communistic, cater to business owners because governments need job created for their citizens to have jobs. Because the government can't create them all. Governments also cater to investors, cause they need the investment capital. Governments cater to businesses by tax write offs. Basically you have tax law but it can be waived for certain exemptions. Business owners get to write off expenses off their taxes that regular employees don't get to use. Business owners can write off just about anything business related, their cars, gas, vacations, meals, etc.. Everybody needs a car to get to work. But only the business owner, or someone who uses a car for commission work, gets to write that off. The tax system is an honor system. Whoever can write off the most, without breaking the law, gets the most. It's actually a goal for a business to not make a profit. Cause if they do, they have to pay tax on profit. So the goal is to spend as much as you can on your cars, meals, vacations, etc., to reduce profit. Which actually, in a way, becomes your salary. This all can be very confusing, that's why you need to be educated of how these things work. Or hire someone who is. We live in a knowledge based economy. If you're poor, the work you do is your tax. If you're rich, it's just numbers on a page. How much goes to government, to you, to employees, etc. Taxes to a rich person are looked at no different than any other expense.

  Now I do believe a Doctor should make more than a cook. A doctor's job is life or death, and is more skilled/educated. Just about anybody can cook a hamburger. But it's also not fair for somebody in business without any formal education to make just as much as a Doctor. Somebody who got a high paying job just because of who they know. And just because somebody cooks a hamburger, doesn't mean they shouldn't have the opportunity to have real ownership in their life. Real wealth is based on what you own, not what you borrow or can borrow. I just think the gap between the rich and poor is too big. It has widened every year since the Great Depression. Our system has gotten more to the point of rewarding people who don't work over people who do.

Trickle-down economics in my opinion doesn't work, in some ways it does. The largest beneficiaries of trickle-down economics are business owners, commission people, and the government. These people benefit the most when times are good. The average person benefits by getting a job but it will still pay just the market value. Which might go up slightly in this time. Why is it called trickle-down? Is it cause wealth trickles down like a water faucet? It's the theory that if you cut a rich person's taxes, they'll spend the extra money back into the economy. Which creates jobs. If trickle-down economics works, then why are people in foreign countries, who work for American companies, being paid $1 an hour? When if the same company did business here, the workers would make $15 an hour. That shows you that the real force at work is supply/demand economics.

Again, real wealth is in what you own, not what you have on loan. The greatest wealth isn't piles of money. It's having the freedom to wake up everyday and do what YOUR heart desires, legally! I've met a lot of close-minded people. That think you have to live by the mold that everybody else does, and just accept it. And I think, how is that freedom? My thought is to do what makes you happy morally as long as you can pay your own way. Most everybody you'll meet in your life will be a hypocrite. Just try not to fall in the trap and think for yourself. If something doesn't make sense, then ask why! People talk about how you should be thankful because you have it better than other people around the world. It's not wrong to be thankful. I just find it to be more slave talk if it's concerning money or a raise. But if they had been thankful and accepted their position at work, they wouldn't be in that higher position. Does giving thanks get you more stuff or gets stuff taken away? I don't think so. Now I'm talking in a work sense here. You should always be thankful for things like your kids, family, and friends!

Money

Since you have to work for money to pay your

bills, you should know how it works. Gold and silver have really been the only true money in the history of the world. Gold is God's form of money, cause it can't be run off a printing press. Gold has always had value cause it's in limited supply. Right now there is enough gold for investment to give every person on the planet 1/3 of an ounce. There is enough silver for investment to give every person on the planet 1/14 of an ounce. When we came off the Gold standard in 1971, gold was around $40 an ounce. At this writing, its around $1700. That's a return of 4,250%. The stock market, dow, was around 850 in 1971. For the dow to have the same return it would have to be around 36,125 today. Which today it's around 13,000 and most of the financial analyst say gold is a bad investment. Gold has always been money because of its scarcity. If you unearthed a treasure chest that was 200 years old, and it had a million dollars each of gold and paper American Continentals. Which one is still worth anything? The continentals are worth nothing because that money system no longer exists. Even though the gold is 200 years old, it is still worth something today. Logic would tell that our money will be worthless one day also.

Governments don't like you using gold because they want you to use their Fiat currency. Fiat means it's not backed by anything real. It's only worth what the collective thinks it's worth. We had a gold backed currency until 1971 and we've had inflation ever since. Inflation happens when more un-backed money is printed, which steals from everybody else. The paper money in your wallet is basically like owning stock, the value of it goes up and down on a daily basis but you just don't see it. When the price of something goes up, it's really the value of your money going down. There are other supply/demand factors in there to. In theory, your paper money could become worthless overnight if all of our creditors (foreign countries) wanted their loans repaid. I don't think this scenario would happen overnight, because the creditor nations would lose also. But I do think this will happen over time. So do you think you're safe because you have money in the bank? Wrong. You need to have some gold and silver to counter the devaluing currency. Are gold and silver a 100% safe bet? No. The government manipulates, any or all, markets under the "Presidents working group on financial markets." Signed by Ronald Reagan in 1987. It legally allows the government to manipulate markets. So we truly don't have free markets but you do have to have something in place to keep markets from totally collapsing in a short period. The stock market is not much different than gambling. You should have professional advice before being in it. Just like anything else, there are people on the inside who know when to buy and sell. Nowhere in the mainstream are you going to find somebody who's going to tell you what the insiders really know. Cause if they did, the insiders wouldn't have the advantage of making money. It's a sucker's game. The only safe way I see is to diversify.

Time after time countries throughout history have gone through hyperinflation. During hyperinflation it could take 1 million dollars to buy a loaf of bread. Basically your money becomes worthless. This has happened many times throughout history. This process makes everybody, except the insiders and the elite, become poor. More fortunes are made during depressions than during economic booms. Because the people on the inside know when to sale, then come back and buy everything pennies on the dollar.

Some people think silver could be the best investment over the next decade. Silver is almost extinct, cause it is used in so many everyday products. Silver also has unique properties that can't be replaced by any other metal. Because of this, some people believe the price of silver will explode. Of course when buying gold and silver coins, or anything, make sure what you're buying is real! There are a lot of fakes out there! Make sure you go through a professional! The thing that could hurt silver is if something cheaper is found to replace its industrial uses.

The Federal Reserve is who runs our monetary system. As said before, whoever controls the money supply, controls the power. The Federal Reserve is not part of the federal government; it's a private bank. The Federal Reserve prints the money for the treasury, and charges interest on that money. Why can't the treasury print our money for free? The Federal Reserve also sets interest rates, which can contract or expand the economy.

So say if no money existed and the Fed prints $1 with interest. Where do you get the second $1 to pay the interest? You have to create another dollar. See, this system is designed to have debt. People are always complaining that we need to pay off the national debt. We can't, it's not possible in theory. The government doesn't care about how much money they spend, cause they'll just print more if they need it.

The system banks use for lending is the fractional reserve system. They are allowed to lend nine times of what is on reserve. If somebody deposit's $10, they can loan $90. Where does the $90 come from? They create the money, out of thin air, by a promissory note. This $90 expands the money supply, which causes more inflation. When that $90 becomes deposited, the bank then can lend $810, and the cycle repeats. You keep creating new money based on the initial $10. So there's always more money loaned than what they have on deposit. Every time you charge on a credit card, you're expanding the money supply. About 10% to 20% of the inflation comes from the government printing money. The majority of inflation comes from banks under the fractional reserve system.

If you have a mortgage, the bank owns your house. You work to pay back your mortgage. The bank paid for your house with made up money, a promissory note. If you don't pay, the bank gets your house back. It's a win-win for the bank. When you look at all the things people are in debt for, it looks just about like the banks own everything.

You can always measure things in a dollar value. For example, a house was $100,000 in 2005 but is now worth $120,000. So the house went up $20,000 in value. But at the same time, gold went up 300%. So in dollar value the house went up in price but when priced in gold, the house went down in value. Gold, silver, corn, wheat, sugar, are real things. Money is just paper. Sometimes if it's printed on paper, it's worth the paper it's printed on. Governments like Fiat money when two countries go to war. Because a gold standard restraints the government's spending. A country using Fiat money can print all the money it needs for war supplies.

Is a house a good investment? At times it is and other times it's not. Some economists say it's a good time to buy a house when interest rates are high. Because when interest rates are high, that usually makes the property value lower and vice versa. Because people base a house on how much they can afford on a monthly payment. You have the monthly payment and the only two variables that can move are the interest rate or overall value. So you buy when the rates are high, which makes the value lower. Then refinance when the rates drop, which lowers your payment but keeps the same payoff. The same would work in reverse. If you bought a house with a low rate and then the rate went up. Your property value most likely would go down or stay the same, unless you have a lot of inflation to counter the deflation. There would also be supply and demand factors also, like anything else.

   People in America are all about owning a house. That if you rent, you're just throwing your money away. That isn't true. There are pros and cons to both. First of all if you have a mortgage on your house, then you don't totally own it. What you have is equity in your house. That you own a portion of your house and the more equity you have, the more you own it. That's a positive that you don't get from renting. But your equity only grows if you're in an up real estate market or if you pay extra on the principal. There are currently a lot of people who are upside down in their mortgages and they can't sell their house. And in some states you can be sued for the difference if your house doesn't bring the money needed during a foreclosure. Then how was that a good investment? They will have paid all this money and will lose everything. That scenario sounds the same as renting to me. A lot of people move every 5-10 years due to job changes. If your job moves you and you can't sell your house, that's not a good thing. Even if you own your house, you totally don't own it cause you have to pay property taxes every year. If you do outright own a house, that's a big advantage over renting. That puts a rent payment back in your pocket every month. Another advantage to renting is that you don't have to do any maintenance and you get amenities like a gym, pool, etc. A disadvantage to renting is that your living space is smaller for the price. Another advantage to renting is you have virtually no commitment and you can easily move anywhere you like. You just pickup and go. But if you find the house of your dreams, it makes you happy, and you can afford it. Then go for it. Just don't fall in the trap that if you don't own a house, you're stupid. Of course hindsight is always twenty-twenty. But I look back on owning a house like; I could have done a lot of things besides owning a house. I could of traveled, went back to school, had more recreation, etc. But at the time I wanted to do the smart thing and own a house. I learned a lot owning a house. You really don't have to buy a house until you have kids in my view.

On a similar note, I'm tired of people who live in a 6000-sqft house say they, or the house, is energy efficient and environmentally friendly! Sounds oxymoronic! If you really cared about being energy efficient and environmentally friendly, wouldn't you live in a 500-sqft house? Or even more than that, in a tent?

Chapter 7:
Everything Else

Physicists have found that it's the natural form of the universe to constantly go from order to disorder. That the most perfect order ever was the start of the Big Bang, and the universe has been going in the direction of disorder ever since. Which made me think about other things. Like the natural order for your house is to be dirty but we constantly clean up, put it back in order, and over time it goes back to disorder. The same is for our bodies. After you're done growing, your body slowly goes to being in disorder. You can use this same analogy in many other things about life. When I see life using this principal, a lot more things make sense. The reason we struggle with so many things is that we're always trying to put something back into order, which is its unnatural state.

One cause of depression is that your body is denying what your brain wants it to do, from a scientific level. We are taught that many of the things our brain wants us to do are wrong. Since everybody is different, everybody thinks different. Of course you have to draw the line somewhere. You can't just do anything your brain desires. For example if you wanted to hurt somebody and you couldn't, that could cause depression but it's also just wrong. I'm just trying to show how many people struggle with wanting to do something they want to do but can't because they've been told it's wrong. Another example is if you wanted to live far away but also wanted to be close to family. You can't do both and either one could cause depression. You just have to find a balance.

I don't believe in taking medications if not necessary. I think you should self heal your body as much as possible, with medicines being a last resort. Some times medicines have side effects and cause you to take more medications, or cause other sickness. Which is more money for drug companies, medicine is a business too! On the other hand, a lot of medicines are lifesavers. Some people argue that medications are nothing more than controlled poisons and that they damage the liver. Your body is powerful at self-healing with the right nutrition and exercise. Think about it; when you get a cut (or any type of illness), the doctor doesn't fix the cut. He assists your body in healing itself. Remember when you see a doctor, dentist, etc. They're in the business of making money too. You have to factor in that in their recommendations. You can't always believe what you're told, but sometimes you have to. In those situations you have to do what you think is best.

Drugs, Drinking, and Driving

Nothing scares me more then thinking of a teen getting behind the wheel of a car. Cars are one, if not the, leading killers among teens. I'm sure we've all known somebody who's died in a car wreck. Kids just don't understand how fragile life really is! How one 5-minute event will change your life forever, and there's no going back! If you're about to drive or just started, drive smart! Don't do stupid driving! Don't do anything because of peer pressure! Especially don't drive fast or stupid during rain or other bad weather conditions. Make sure you have good tires on your car. I've had a wreck before. Driving normal but wrecked because the baldness on my tires. That alone could have ended my life or somebody else's. Don't believe that anything bad can't happen to you because some angel is watching over you, because they're not. You could go out the door this second, have a wreck, and die. So always tell your loved ones you love them, because you may not get a second chance. I've witnessed this. Talk to somebody one second and they hit a tree on the way home. Never drive under the influence of drugs, prescription or not, or alcohol. And always wear your seatbelt! You never know when somebody's on prescription drugs, driving down the road, cross's the line, and hits you head on even though you've done nothing wrong.

You're young, just started driving, have some drinks with friends, having a good time, hit another car head on, on the way home, and in the other car you just killed a four-year-old. You go to jail for a time, but what you took from these parents can never be replaced. They, and you, will have to live with this loss the rest of your lives! This four-year-old never got to go to college, never got married, never had kids, never got to do a lot of things. The parents will always think if they could of just taken the other route, left 5 minutes earlier, or 5 minutes later. Think about this every time you drive a car, cause it happens to somebody every day!

I know how peer pressure is! You're told growing up not to do a lot of bad things, pretty simple. Before you know it, everybody's doing those very things. From the jocks to the nerds, and nobody wants you around if you're not doing what everybody else is doing. I know it can be hard but you have to do what's smart! Because none of your friends will be there for you when you fall! They'll go on and party without you. Peer pressure doesn't get any easier when you get older. Whatever you do, ignore peer pressure! This goes for adults as well. Studies have shown that people who drink get better jobs, on average, than people who don't. Because they socialize more, get to know more people, and have more connections. How sad!

Never try drugs! There are some drugs you do once and you're hooked. It's not worth it; you don't want to go down that road! Don't even try drugs once, unless you plan for your life to go down the drain. That also includes prescription drugs!

Death

On the subject of death, I've never lost a real close loved one and hope I don't for a long time! People grieve, some longer than others. Of course there has to be time for grieving and some will grieve the rest of their life. My view is somewhat of a cold one. The person that has passed away is never coming back. No matter what you do, they're never coming back. No matter how much you pray or how hard you grieve, they're never coming back. You just have to move on with your life the best you can. Every minute your own life is getting shorter. In some ways you're just wasting time and energy. I know it's cold but it's just how it is. People want to believe the person is watching them from above. It makes them feel better. In reality, we just really don't know where this person's soul is. We could go to heaven or go into nothingness, we don't 100% know. I personally believe in an afterlife. I can't believe this whole experience is for nothing, but I also believe there isn't a hell. How could a fair and just God send anybody to hell? Could any parent send his or her kid to hell? And if it's a choice, I choose not to go to Hell!

Suicide

Suicide has to be one of the dumbest things a person can do! I had a friend who committed suicide. He didn't want to get old. He wasn't old anyways; he was just in his 20s. He must have had something wrong with him. You would have to have something wrong with you to want to commit suicide! Nothing in life is worth killing yourself over! No job, no spouse, nothing! Some people kill themselves to get back at somebody. How dumb is that? If you commit suicide, life goes on for everybody else. You think people care you killed yourself? Cause they don't, they'll probably just laugh about it years later. You just simply don't have that kind of power over other people. Nobody cares about you. You just have to go and do what makes you happy. Cause if you think your suicide affects somebody, it doesn't. Nobody cares.

On the same note, nothing in life is also not worth killing somebody else over. No spouse, no job, no situation. Cause you'll spend the rest of your life in jail. The person you killed, their family will have to live with the death the rest of their lives. Don't do it, it's not worth it! In most situations you come across, just walk away. Don't get hot-headed over every little thing. Do what's smart for you! Sometimes you do have to stand up for yourself, but you also don't want to get yourself killed! The point in life is to survive. There's no point in arguing with people! It hardly changes minds. Just tell people what they want to hear and go do what you want to do, legally!

.

In Closing:

First of all, I want to thank you for ready my book. I'm sure there are things in here that people will disagree with or get mad at. That's not the point of writing this book. Of course this book is though my perspective on how I see the world. I try to be as honest as possible and tell you things that people think about but will not tell you. One objective is to pull back that curtain. The thing is, you think you know a person but you never know 100% what's in their mind. The only thing you 100% know is what's in your mind. My goal is not for you to get mad about the book. My goal is for you to use this information and better yourself! You always hear people say, "I wish I knew then what I know now!" Maybe this book will save people the time it took me to figure all these things out? People constantly play things over and over in their mind, I guess constantly hoping they could have changed something or try to figure out why something happened. I don't want to give people the idea that they can learn from this book and go out and mistreat people. I do believe you should be honest and loyal to your family and close friends. But for the general public, you have to use a different set of rules. When you go and see a Doctor, you expect that person to be more of a professional at Doctor than you are. When somebody says they're a Christian, you expect that person to lead a better life. Which isn't always the case, in a lot of cases you find the person to be no different than anybody else. I don't want to totally knock Religion. They do, do good work for people who struggle with drugs, alcohol, people who need guidance, etc. People join Religions for many different reasons, some good and some bad.

Whether you have problems cause your parents divorce, you lost a loved one, broke up with a spouse, lost a job, didn't follow a dream, etc.. You have to get past what's in your past! You have to start from now! If you have the will power, you can change anything in your control! And nobodies going to do it for you. Also know if you feel the way I do, you are not alone! Thank You!

Made in the USA
San Bernardino, CA
04 September 2017